Discover
Heavy Equipment

by Amanda Trane

© 2017 by Amanda Trane
ISBN: 978-1-53240-2616
eISBN: 978-1-53240-2623
Images licensed from Fotolia.com
All rights reserved.
No portion of this book may be reproduced
without express permission of the publisher.
First Edition
Published in the United States by
Xist Publishing
www.xistpublishing.com
PO Box 61593 Irvine, CA 92602

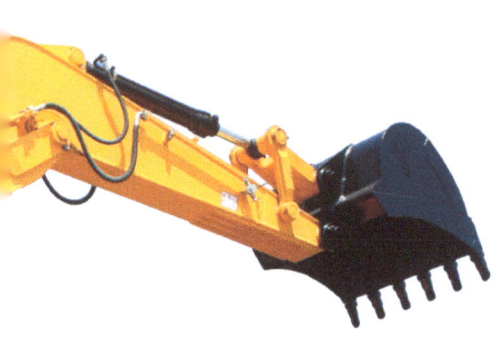

Heavy Equipment makes big jobs easier.

Before people made tractors, every job had to be done by people or animals.

5

Tractors help farmers grow more food.

Today, most farmers use tractors to get their fields ready to plant.

Some farm tractors are fancy. This tractor has air conditioning.

Farmers are not the only people to use heavy equipment.

14

Some families own small tractors or riding mowers. Almost anyone can mow the grass on a lawn tractor.

Construction workers use heavy equipment all day. An excavator is used to dig.

This is a tractor with a backhoe. It has a bucket and a loader.

This bulldozer can push dirt or sand with the front blade.

A road roller makes the ground flat. People use it to build roads and to get ready to start buildings.

Forklifts carry heavy items from one place to another. The metal forks carry items inside or outside.

Some heavy equipment has four wheels.

This red farm tractor has eight wheels.

Some heavy equipment has tracks instead of wheels.

Heavy equipment helps people do big jobs faster.